D0915580

READING POWER

American Tycoons

John D. Rockefeller

and the Oil Industry

Lewis K. Parker

The Rosen Publishing Group's
PowerKids Press™
New York

Published in 2003 by The Rosen Publishing Group, Inc.
29 East 21st Street, New York, NY 10010

First Edition

Book Design: Daniel Hosek

Photo Credits: Cover, pp. 12–13, 19 Library of Congress, Prints and Photographs Division; pp. 4, 5, 7, 8, 9, 10–11, 15, 16, 21 courtesy of the Rockefeller Archive Center; pp.12 (inset), 17 © Bettman/Corbis; p. 14 Science, Industry and Business Library, The New York Public Library, Astor, Lenox and Tilden Foundations; p. 18 © Underwood & Underwood/Corbis; p. 20 © Stan Wayman/TimePix

Library of Congress Cataloging-in-Publication Data

Parker, Lewis K.
John D. Rockefeller and the oil industry / Lewis K. Parker.
    p. cm. — (American tycoons)
Summary: A brief biography of American oil magnate, John D. Rockefeller.
ISBN 0-8239-6446-9 (lib. bdg.)
1. Rockefeller, John D. (John Davison), 1839-1937—Juvenile
literature. 2. Capitalists and financiers—United
States—Biography—Juvenile literature. 3. Industrialists—United
States—Biography—Juvenile literature. 4. Philanthropists—United
States—Biography—Juvenile literature. [1. Rockefeller, John D. (John
Davison), 1839-1937. 2. Capitalists and financiers. 3.
Philanthropists.] I. Title.
CT275.R75 P37 2003
338.7'6223382'092—dc21

                                2002000139

]

Contents

The Beginning

Today, oil is used for many things. It can be used to power machines, heat houses, make paints and plastics, and much more. However, in the 1800s, oil was mainly used to light lamps. John D. Rockefeller helped to change the way people used oil. He found many new uses for it.

John Davison Rockefeller was born in Richford, New York, on July 8, 1839.

The Rockefeller family lived on a farm in Richford, New York. In 1853, they moved to Cleveland, Ohio.

John D. Rockefeller (right) had five brothers and sisters. Here, he is sitting with his brother, William (left), and his sister, Mary Ann (middle).

John Rockefeller went to high school in Cleveland, Ohio. He was very good at math and was able to do hard arithmetic problems in his head. But Rockefeller didn't finish high school. Instead, he took business classes at a local college.

Rockefeller was only sixteen years old when he got a job as a bookkeeper.

> "I cannot remember when hard work was new or strange to me. We were taught to work, to save, and to give."
> —John D. Rockefeller

Rockefeller worked hard his entire life to make his fortune.

7

Family

When Rockefeller was twenty-five years old, he married Laura Spelman, a teacher. John and Laura Rockefeller had five children—Elizabeth, Alice, Alta, Edith, and John D., Jr.

Laura Spelman Rockefeller

John D. Rockefeller

Pictured here are the Rockefeller children (from left to right): Alta, Elizabeth, Edith, and John D., Jr. Alice died when she was a baby.

The Oil Business

The Industrial Revolution created a need for new kinds of energy. Rockefeller believed that oil would be this form of energy. In 1863, Rockefeller and some of his friends started an oil refinery business in Cleveland. Two years later, it was one of the largest oil refineries in the area. By 1865, Rockefeller owned the company.

One of Rockefeller's earliest oil businesses was Rockefeller & Andrews. Rockefeller started the business with his friend Samuel Andrews.

11

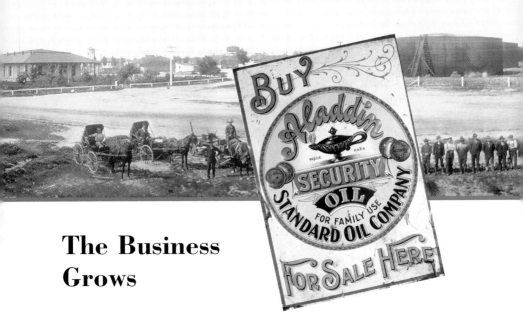

The Business Grows

In 1870, Rockefeller started the Standard Oil Company of Ohio with his brother and four other men. Then, he started buying other oil companies in Cleveland and other cities, such as New York. Standard Oil became a very large, successful company.

Check It Out

Rockefeller used the waste from refining oil. The waste was used to make many things, such as gasoline and paraffin.

Rockefeller stored his oil in big tanks.

From Crude Oil to Everyday Use

Refineries clean crude oil, the oil that comes out of the ground. Then, gas, wax, and many more things are made.

Crude Oil

Oil Refinery

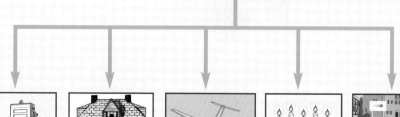

Gasoline   Home Heating Oil   Jet Fuel   Wax   Asphalt

As Standard Oil continued to buy more companies, fewer oil companies were left. Standard Oil wanted all the oil business.

Many people said this was unfair. They thought that Standard Oil was buying up other companies so it could control the oil industry.

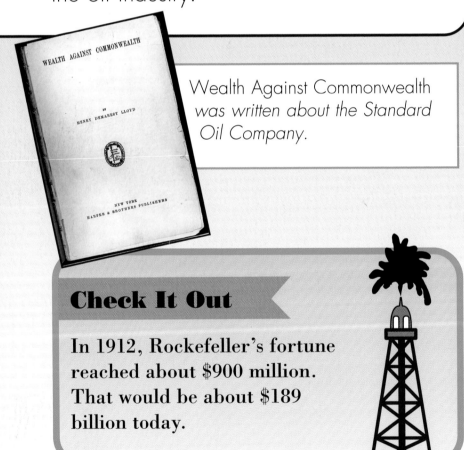

Wealth Against Commonwealth *was written about the Standard Oil Company.*

Check It Out

In 1912, Rockefeller's fortune reached about $900 million. That would be about $189 billion today.

Rockefeller's success made him well-known around the world.

15

In 1890, Standard Oil was sued in court for its unfair control of the oil industry. Two years later, the court in Ohio decided that Standard Oil was a monopoly *(muh-NA-puh-lee)*. The court made Standard Oil break into several smaller companies.

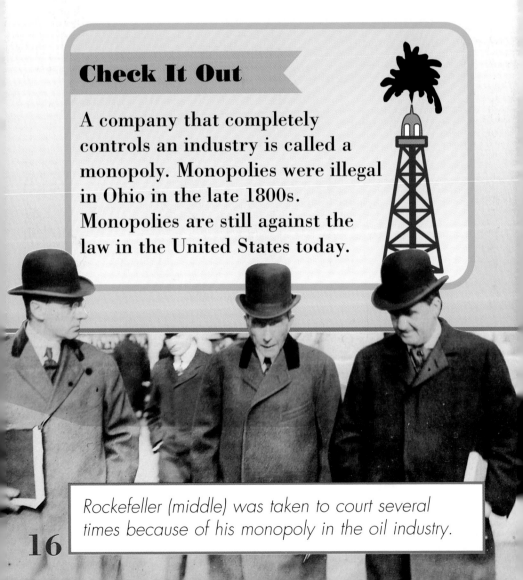

Check It Out

A company that completely controls an industry is called a monopoly. Monopolies were illegal in Ohio in the late 1800s. Monopolies are still against the law in the United States today.

Rockefeller (middle) was taken to court several times because of his monopoly in the oil industry.

Rockefeller later brought his smaller companies together to form the Standard Oil Company of New Jersey. In 1911, the U.S. Supreme Court decided that this company was also illegal.

Helping Others

All his life, Rockefeller gave money to those in need. He used his money to help people in many different ways. He helped many schools and gave money to scientists to find cures for diseases.

Rockefeller died on May 23, 1937, after giving away more than $530 million in his lifetime.

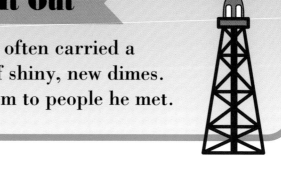

Check It Out

Rockefeller often carried a pocketful of shiny, new dimes. He gave them to people he met.

Time Line

July 8, 1839	1855	1863
John D. Rockefeller is born	Gets first job as bookkeeper	Starts first oil business

Rockefeller gave millions of dollars to help start the University of Chicago.

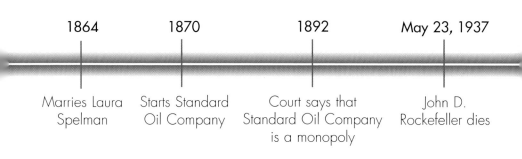

1864	1870	1892	May 23, 1937
Marries Laura Spelman	Starts Standard Oil Company	Court says that Standard Oil Company is a monopoly	John D. Rockefeller dies

John D. Rockefeller was ahead of his time. He found new and important ways to use oil. Rockefeller's hard work and goodwill changed the lives of many people around the world.

Following his grandfather's example, Nelson Rockefeller also worked to help others. He was the vice president of the United States from 1974 to 1977.

I was early taught to work as well as play;
My life has been one long, happy holiday—
Full of work, and full of play—
I dropped the worry on the way—
And God was good to me every day.
                    —John D. Rockefeller

Glossary

asphalt (**as**-fawlt) a black, tarlike product that is used to make roads

bookkeeper (**buk**-kee-puhr) someone who keeps records for a business

college (**kahl**-ihj) a school where people can study after high school

cures (**kyurz**) drugs or treatments that make someone better

diseases (dih-**zeez**-uhz) illnesses

goodwill (gud-**wihl**) kindness or cheerfulness

Industrial Revolution (ihn-**duhs**-tree-uhl rehv-uh-**loo**-shuhn) a slow change from hand-made tools and home manufacturing to power-driven tools and large-scale factory production

industry (**ihn**-duh-stree) a kind of business that makes a particular product, usually in a factory

paraffin (**par**-uh-fihn) waxy matter made from wood, coal, or oil that is used in candles and other things

refinery (rih-**fy**-nuhr-ee) a place where oil is heated to make it pure

Resources

Books

John D. Rockefeller: Oil Baron and Philanthropist
by Rosemary Coughlin
Morgan Reynolds (2001)

John D. Rockefeller: Richest Man Ever
by Ellen Greenman Coffey
Blackbirch (2001)

Web Sites

Due to the changing nature of Internet links, PowerKids Press has developed an on-line list of Web sites related to the subjects of this book. This site is updated regularly. Please use this link to access the list:

http://www.powerkidslinks.com/aty/jdr/

Index

Word Count: 492

Note to Librarians, Teachers, and Parents

If reading is a challenge, Reading Power is a solution! Reading Power is perfect for readers who want high-interest subject matter at an accessible reading level. These fact-filled, photo-illustrated books are designed for readers who want straightforward vocabulary, engaging topics, and a manageable reading experience. With clear picture/text correspondence, leveled Reading Power books put the reader in charge. Now readers have the power to get the information they want and the skills they need in a user-friendly format.